Mediterranea Mastery

Proven Strategies On How To Loss Weight With Mediterranean Diet Meal Plan To Detox The Body.

Written By

HOLLIE MCCARTHY, RDN

Table of Contents

INTRODUCTION 9

BREAKFAST 11

    Very Vanilla French Toast (Vegan).. 12

    French toast With Caramel Apple Topping (Vegan) 13

    Peanut Butter And Banana–Stuffed French Toast (Vegan) 15

    Granola-Infused Oatmeal (Vegan)... 17

LUNCH... 19

    Fresh bell pepper basil pizzaSERVES: 2.. 20

    Low carb pasta a la carbonara 23

DINNER 25

    Orange and sage glazed duck breast... 26

    Perfect ribeye steak... 28

SNACKS 31

    Salted caramel glazed maple bacon cake pops 32

    Coconut cream yogurt.. 34

SIDE DISHES 37

    Cheesy creamed spinach 38

    Delicious vegetable medley.. 39

DESSERT... 41

    Baked Bananas with A Twist Of Lime 42

    Blushing Poached Pears.. 44

    Grilled Orange And Strawberry Skewers 46

    Rum-Sautéed Pineapple and Bananas With Toasted Coconut And Pecans
.... 47

    Nellie's Peachy Melba... 48

Asian Flavors Fruit Bowl 50

Sweet Polenta With Grilled Pineapple And Strawberry Sauce 51

Pineapple Couscous Timbales with Blueberry Sauce............................ 53

Lime-Macerated Mangos 54

MEDITERRANEAN SEAFOOD 55

Dad's Mussels.. 56

Oysters grilled with roasted garlic butter and romano 57

Baked Oysters with Bleu Cheese... 59

Barbecued Oysters 61

Fried Oysters 62

Oysters Johnny Reb.. 63

Oysters Rockefeller 65

Pan-fried Oysters 66

Scalloped Oysters 67

Corn Bread Fried Oysters 68

Thai-style Mango Salad with Griddled Prawns 69

Spicy Thai Curry.. 71

Pesto-stuffed prawns with guacamole vinaigrette 73

Tempura Prawns 75

MEDITERRANEAN PASTA 77

Pasta Sausage Skillet 78

Gilroy Garlic Spaghetti 80

30-Minute Spaghetti Skillet... 82

Autumn Vegetable Roast 84

Homemade Chinese Hot and Sour Soup.. 87

Full Indonesian Stir Fry 89

VEGAN MAIN DISHES 91

Almost One-Dish Thanksgiving Dinner.. 92

Seitan Milanese with Panko And Lemon 94

Sesame-Crusted Seitan... 95

Pan-Seared Seitan With Artichokes And Olives... 96

Seitan With Ancho-Chipotle Sauce... 98

Seitan Piccata.. 100

672 - Three-Seed Seitan 102

Fajitas without Borders 104

Seitan with Green Apple Relish 106

COOKING CONVERSION CHART... 107

INTRODUCTION

Thank you for purchasing this book!

The Mediterranean diet is **a complete and balanced diet ideal for those who want to lose weight or maintain it**: it is **low in fat, mostly unsaturated, rich in low-calorie density foods, provides a lot of fiber that promotes satiety**, so - with quantities modulated on your needs - it is also perfect to get back in shape. Also because **it is a varied diet, never monotonous, rich in tasty dishes**, three important elements for those who follow a low-calorie diet to lose weight.

The Mediterranean diet is healthy recommended also during pregnancy. **It helps to contain weight gain, protecting the future mother from the risk of metabolic complications**. Among these, **gestational diabetes**, which can have serious consequences both for her health and for that of the baby. Following this diet can also be useful to women who enter pregnancy with problems of pre-existing obesity, chronic hypertension, or increased lipid levels.

Enjoy your reading!

BREAKFAST

Very Vanilla French Toast (Vegan)

SERVES: 4

INGREDIENTS

- 1 (12-ounce) package firm silken tofu, drained
- 1½ cups soy milk
- 2 tablespoons cornstarch
- 1 tablespoon canola or grapeseed oil
- 2 teaspoons sugar
- 1½ teaspoons pure vanilla extract
- ¼ teaspoon salt
- slices day-old Italian bread
- Canola or grapeseed oil, for frying

DIRECTIONS

1. Preheat the oven to 225°F. In a blender or food processor, combine the tofu, soy milk, cornstarch, oil, sugar, vanilla, and salt and blend until smooth.
2. Pour the batter into a shallow bowl and dip the bread in the batter, turning to coat both sides.
3. On a griddle or large skillet, heat a thin layer of oil over medium heat. Place the French toast on the hot griddle and cook until golden brown on both sides, turning once, 3 to 4 minutes per side.
4. Transfer the cooked French toast to a heatproof platter and keep warm in the oven while cooking the rest.

French toast With Caramel Apple Topping (Vegan)

SERVES: 4

INGREDIENTS

- ½ cup plus 2 teaspoons light brown sugar
- tablespoons vegan margarine
- Granny Smith apples, peeled, cored, and cut into ¼-inch slices
- ½ cup pure maple syrup
- 1 cup soy milk
- ⅓ cup all-purpose flour
- ½ teaspoon ground cinnamon
- 1½ teaspoons pure vanilla extract
- 6 slices of bread of choice
- Canola or grapeseed oil, for frying

DIRECTIONS

1. Preheat the oven to 225°F. In a large skillet, heat ½ cup of the sugar over medium-low heat. Cook,

2. stirring constantly, until the sugar melts and begins to caramelize. Add the margarine and continue stirring to blend. Add the apple slices and stir to coat. Add the maple syrup and simmer over low heat until tender, stirring occasionally for about 7 minutes. Remove from heat and cover to keep warm.

3. In a shallow bowl, whisk together the soy milk, flour, cinnamon, vanilla, and the remaining 2 teaspoons of sugar. Dip the bread in the batter, turning to coat both sides.

4. On a griddle or large skillet, heat a thin layer of oil over medium heat. Place the French toast on the griddle and cook until golden on both sides, turning once, 3 to 4 minutes per side.

5. Transfer the cooked French toast to a heatproof platter and keep warm in the oven while cooking the rest. Serve with the apple topping.

Peanut Butter And Banana–Stuffed French Toast (Vegan)

SERVES: 4

INGREDIENTS

- 1 ripe banana
- ½ cup creamy peanut butter
- ¼ cup light brown sugar
- 2 teaspoons pure maple syrup
- 6 slices French bread or 8 slices Italian bread, cut into ½-inch slices
- 1 cup soy milk
- tablespoons all-purpose flour
- 1 teaspoon pure vanilla extract
- 2 tablespoons vegan margarine, plus more if needed

DIRECTIONS

1. In a medium bowl, mash the banana. Add the peanut butter, sugar, and maple syrup, stirring to mix well. Preheat the oven to 225°F.

2. Spread 1 to 2 tablespoons of the peanut butter-banana mixture onto half of the bread slices, then top each with one of the remaining bread slices.

3. In a shallow bowl, whisk together the soy milk, flour, and vanilla. Place a sandwich in the batter. Let it soak for about 5 seconds. Turn the sandwich over and let it soak another 5 seconds. Repeat with the remaining sandwiches.

4. On a griddle or large skillet, melt the margarine over medium heat. Cook the stuffed bread slices until golden brown on both sides, about 4 minutes per side. Transfer the cooked French toast warm to a heatproof platter and keep warm in the oven while cooking the rest.

Granola-Infused Oatmeal (Vegan)

SERVES: 4 to 6

INGREDIENTS

- cups water
- 1¾ cups old-fashioned oats
- 1 teaspoon ground cinnamon
- ¼ teaspoon salt
- ¾ cup vegan granola, homemade (see Granola) or store-bought

DIRECTIONS

1. In a large saucepan, bring the water to a boil over high heat. Reduce the heat to low, stir in the oats, cinnamon, and salt.
2. Simmer for 5 minutes, stirring occasionally.
3. Remove from the heat and stir in the granola. Cover and let stand for about 3 minutes before serving.

LUNCH

Fresh bell pepper basil pizzaSERVES: 2

INGREDIENTS

Pizza Base

Toppings

- 4 oz. Shredded Cheddar Cheese
- 1 medium Vine Tomato
- 1/4 cup Rao's Tomato Sauce
- 2/3 medium Bell Pepper
- 2-3 tbsp. Fresh Chopped
- Basil

DIRECTIONS

1. Preheat oven to 400F. Start by measuring out all of your dry spices and flours in a bowl. 1/2 cup Almond Flour, 2 tbsp. Psyllium Husk, 2 tbsp. Fresh Parmesan Cheese, 1 tsp. Italian Seasoning, 1/2 tsp. Salt, and 1/2 tsp. Pepper.

2. Measure out 6 oz. Mozzarella Cheese into a bowl.

3. Microwave the cheese for 40-50 seconds until it's completely melted and pliable with your hands. Add 2 tbsp. Cream Cheese to the top.

4. Add 1 egg to the dry ingredients and mix a little bit.

5. Add the melted mozzarella cheese and cream cheese to the egg and dry ingredients and mix everything. Don't mind getting your hands dirty here – they'll be the best tool for the job. You'll get a bit messy, but it'll be oh so worth it in the end.

6. Break the dough into 2 equal (or almost equal) portions. Roll the dough out quite thin – a little under 1/ Here, you can use the top of a pot or other large round object to cut out your pizza base. You can form the circles by hand, but

7. I'm not a very smart person and mine always turns out oval. When I work with this, I always like to work on top of a Silpat because it's naturally non-stick.

8. Fold the edges of the dough inward and form a small crust on the dough. If you have any scraps remaining, you can add them to the crust if you want.

9. Bake the dough for 10 minutes. Just enough so they're starting to get slightly golden brown.

10. Remove the crust from the oven and let cool for a moment.

11. Slice a medium vine tomato and put half on each pizza along with 2 tbsp. tomato sauce per pizza.

12. Top these suckers with cheese – about 2 oz. Shredded Cheddar per pizza.

13. Chop up the bell peppers. You can use 1 bell pepper or 2 different colors. I am using 1/3 red bell pepper and 1/3 yellow bell pepper for the topping.

14. Arrange the peppers how you like and throw them back in the oven for another 8-10 minutes.

15. Remove the pizzas from the oven and let them cool. In the meantime, slice up some fresh basil and have it ready for serving.

16. Serve it up – top with fresh basil and enjoy the fresh bites of summer!

NUTRITIONAL VALUES

410 Calories, 33g Fats, 3g Net Carbs, and 28g Protein.

Low carb pasta a la carbonara

SERVES: 3

INGREDIENTS

- 400 gr Pasta
- 5 Oz. Bacon
- 2 large Egg Yolks
- 1 large Egg
- 1 tbsp. Heavy Cream
- 1/3 cup Fresh Grated Parmesan (Plus garnish)
- 3 tbsp. Fresh Chopped Basil
- Fresh Ground Black Pepper to Taste

DIRECTIONS

1. Prepare pasta
2. Freeze bacon for 15 minutes prior for easier cutting. Slice bacon into small cubes and cook until crisp over high heat.
3. Set bacon aside to cool on paper towels and become even crispier.
4. Save 1/3 bacon grease and keep the other 2/3 in the pan. Mix 1 large egg and 2 large egg yolks.
5. Measure out 1/3 cup freshly grated parmesan cheese.
6. Add parmesan, cream, and saved 1/3 bacon grease that was saved to the egg and egg yolk mixture. Stir together well until a thick sauce is formed.
7. Cook pasta in a pan with the bacon grease that is leftover high heat.
8. Add pasta to a mixing bowl, and then add crisped bacon and toss.

9. Add carbonara sauce to the pasta along with 2 tbsp. freshly chopped basil and fresh cracked black pepper. Mix until all strands of pasta are covered completely.

10. Garnish with extra fresh cracked black pepper and chopped basil.

NUTRITIONAL VALUES

553 Calories, 44g Fats, 8g Net Carbs, and 27g Protein.

DINNER

Orange and sage glazed duck breast

SERVES: 1

INGREDIENTS

- 1 6 OZ. Duck Breast
- 2 tbsp. Butter
- 1 tbsp. Heavy Cream
- 1 tbsp. Swerve Sweetener
- 1/2 tsp. Orange Extract
- 1/4 tsp. Sage
- 1 cup Spinach

DIRECTIONS

1   Score the duck skin on top of the breast.

2   Season duck breast on both sides with salt and pepper.

3   In a pan over medium-low heat, add butter and swerve. Let this cook down until the butter has slightly browned.

4   Once the butter has turned a dark golden color, add sage and orange extract.

5   Let this cook until butter is a deep amber color.

6   In the meantime, put the duck breast into a cold pan. Set the heat of the pan to medium-high on the stove.

7   After a few minutes, flip the duck breast and see the delicious crisp skin.

8   Add heavy cream to the orange and sage butter, then stir together well. Pour this over the duck breast in the pan and let mix with the duck fat. Cook for a few minutes longer.

9   Wilt some spinach in the pan you used to make the sauce.

10   Let the duck rest for 2-3 minutes, then slice and place on top of wilted spinach with sauce.

11

NUTRITIONAL VALUES

798 Calories, 71g Fats, 0g Net Carbs, and 36g Protein.

Perfect ribeye steak

SERVES: 2

INGREDIENTS

- 16 oz. Ribeye Steak (1 – 1 1/4 inch thick)
- 1 tbsp. Duck Fat (or other high smoke point oil like Peanut Oil)
- 1 tbsp. Butter
- 1/2 tsp. Thyme, chopped
- Salt and Pepper to Taste

DIRECTIONS

1 Preheat oven to 400F. Put your cast iron skillet in the oven while it's cold so

2 Prep your steak by rubbing with a light coating of duck fat or oil. Then, apply a healthy coating of salt and pepper on all sides including the edges.

3 Once the oven is pre-heated, remove the cast iron skillet and place it on the stovetop over medium heat. Add duck fat, or oil, and put your steak into the pan and let sear. Do this for 1 1/2 to 2 minutes.

4 Flip the steak and put it into the oven immediately for 4-6 minutes (depending on doneness – 4 minutes for medium-rare). Prepare for a bit of smoke to happen as the pan is very hot – but once it goes back into the oven, it should cool down slightly and stop smoking.

5 Measure out 2 tbsp. butter and 1/2 tsp. chopped thyme.

6   Take the steak out of the oven and place it on the stovetop over low heat. Add the butter to the pan and base the steak with the butter. Push the handle of the cast iron downward (you may need something to protect your hand) and scoop the butter up with a spoon, ladling it over the steak. Do this for 2-4 minutes depending on the doneness you want.

7   Place in foil or cover, and let rest for 5 minutes.

8   Serve up with your favorite veggies and extra butter if you'd like!

NUTRITIONAL VALUES

750 Calories, 66g Fats, 0g Net Carbs, and 38g Protein.

SNACKS

Salted caramel glazed maple bacon cake pops

SERVES: 4

INGREDIENTS

- Maple Bacon Cake Pops
- 6 Oz. Burgers' Smokehouse Country Bacon
- 5 large eggs, separated 1/4 cup Maple Syrup
- 1/2 tsp. Vanilla Extract 1/4 Cup NOW Erythritol 1/4 tsp. Liquid Stevia
- 1 cup Honeyville Almond Flour
- 2 tbsp. Psyllium Husk Powder
- 1 tsp. Baking Powder
- 2 tbsp. Butter
- 1/2 tsp. Cream of Tartar
- Salted Caramel Glaze 5 tbsp. Butter
- 5 tbsp. Heavy Cream
- 2 1/2 tbsp. Torani Sugar-Free Salted Caramel

DIRECTIONS

1. Slice 6 Oz. Burgers' Smokehouse Country Bacon into small bite-size chunks.

2. Either freezing the bacon for 30 minutes prior, or using scissors normally helps with this process.

3. Heat a pan to medium-high heat and cook the bacon until crisp.

4. Once crisp, remove the bacon from the pan and allow to dry on paper towels. Save excess bacon grease to sauté vegetables or other meats in it.

5. Preheat oven to 325F. In 2 separate bowls, separate the egg yolks from the egg whites of 5 large eggs.

6. In the bowl with the egg yolks, add 1/4 cup maple syrup, 1/4 cup erythritol, 1/4 tsp. liquid stevia, and 1/2 tsp. vanilla extract.

7. Using a hand mixer, mix this for about 2 minutes. The egg yolks should become lighter in color.

8. Add 1 cup Honeyville almond flour, 2 tbsp. Psyllium husk powder, 2 tbsp. butter, and 1 tsp. baking powder.

9. Mix this again until a thick batter forms.

10. Wash off the whisks of the hand mixer in the sink to make sure all traces of fats are washed off of the whisks.

11. Add 1/2 tsp. cream of tartar to the egg whites.

12. Whisk the egg whites using a hand mixer until solid peaks form.

13. Add 2/3 crisped bacon into the cake pop batter.

14. Add about 1/3 of the egg whites into the batter and aggressively mix.

Coconut cream yogurt

SERVES: 1

INGREDIENTS

- 1 can Full Fat Coconut Milk
- 2 capsules NOW Probiotic-10
- 1/2 tsp. NOW Xanthan Gum (1/4 tsp. split between both jars)
- 2/3 cup Heavy Whipping Cream
- Toppings of Your Choice

DIRECTIONS

1. Open a can of coconut milk and stir it well. You want to make sure the cream and water in the can is thoroughly mixed.
2. Put the coconut milk into whatever container you'd like. I separated mine into 2 200mL mason jars. Have your NOW Probiotic-10 handy.
3. Turn your oven light on and place the jars in the oven. Close the oven door, keeping the light on, and let it sit for 12-24 hours overnight. The longer the bacteria can culture, the thicker the mixture will get, but it doesn't make too big of a difference.
4. Empty your entire yogurt into a mixing bowl and sprinkle 1/2 tsp. Xanthan gum over it. Using a hand mixer, mix this well.
5. In a separate bowl, whip up 2/3 cup heavy cream until stiff peaks form. You want this to be solid cream almost.
6. Dump the solid cream into the yogurt and mix at a low speed until the consistency you want is achieved.

7. Add toppings, flavorings, or fillings of your choice, and enjoy!

Usually, yogurt has a serving size of 1/2 cup, but you will get just over 1/2 cup per serving with this.

NUTRITIONAL VALUES

315 Calories, 33g Fats, 3g Net Carbs and 0g Protein.

SIDE DISHES

Cheesy creamed spinach

SERVES: 1

INGREDIENTS

- Cups Spinach
- 1 1/2 Cups Cheddar Cheese
- 3 Tbsp. Butter
- 3 Tbsp. Heavy Cream
- 1/2 tsp. Mrs. Dash Table Blend
- 1/2 tsp. Salt
- 1/2 tsp. Pepper

DIRECTIONS

1 Start to melt 3 Tbsp. Butter in a pan over medium-low heat.

2 While the butter is melting, grate 1 1/2 Cups Cheddar Cheese.

3 Add 7 cups of spinach to the pan once the butter has melted, then add seasonings: 1/2 tsp. Salt, 1/2 tsp. Pepper, and 1/2 tsp. Mrs. Dash Table Blend.

4 Once the spinach is wilted, add 1 1/2 Cup Cheddar Cheese and 3 Tbsp.

5 Heavy Cream.

6 Mix everything well and let all of the sauce meltdowns.

7 Move the spinach to one side of the pan and turn the heat to medium-high.

8 Let the sauce reduce.

9 Once the sauce has reduced some, mix everything again.

10 Serve hot! This pairs well with the Paprika Chicken Recipe!

Delicious vegetable medley

SERVES: 4

INGREDIENTS

- Tbsp. Olive Oil
- 240g Baby Bella Mushrooms
- 115g Broccoli
- 100g Sugar Snap Peas
- 90g Bell Pepper
- 90g Spinach
- 2 Tbsp. Pumpkin Seeds
- 2 tsp. Minced Garlic
- 1 tsp. Salt
- 1 tsp. Pepper
- 1/2 tsp. Red Pepper Flake

DIRECTIONS

1   Start by prepping all your vegetables. Slice the 115g broccoli into bite-size florets. Chop the 90g bell pepper in strips and then chop the strips down. If you're not using pre-sliced mushrooms, make sure to slice your 240g mushrooms here also.

2   Add 6 Tbsp. Olive Oil to a wok and bring to hot heat.

3   Once the oil is hot, add garlic and let it cook for 1 minute.

4   Once the garlic starts to brown, add mushrooms and stir together.

5   Once the mushrooms have soaked up most of the oil, add broccoli and mix everything well.

6   Add 100g Sugar Snap Peas to the mixture and stir well.

7   Add your peppers to the dish and stir it up well. You want the peppers to still be a bit crunchy by the time you finish.

8   Add all of your seasoning: 1 tsp. Salt, 1 tsp. Pepper, and 1/2 tsp. Red Pepper Flakes. Taste here and add more spices if you want.

9   Add 2 Tbsp. Pumpkin Seeds and stir them into the vegetables.

10 Once the vegetables are cooked, put 90g spinach on top of the vegetables and let the steam wilt them down.

11 Once the spinach is wilted, mix everything and serve!

DESSERT

Baked Bananas with A Twist Of Lime

SERVES: 4

INGREDIENTS

- 2 or 3 limes
- 2 tablespoons light brown sugar
- ⅓ cup water
- ripe bananas
- 2 tablespoons vegan margarine
- 2 tablespoons crushed unsalted roasted cashews or peanuts
- 2 tablespoons shredded sweetened coconut

DIRECTIONS

1   Preheat the oven to 350°F. Use a channel zester to remove 4 long strips of peel from the limes. Twist the strips and set them aside to use as garnish. Juice and zest the limes to yield 2 tablespoons of juice and 1 teaspoon of fine zest. Set aside.

2   In a small saucepan, combine the sugar and water and bring to a boil. Reduce heat to low and simmer for 30 seconds, stirring to dissolve the sugar. Remove from the heat and add the reserved lime juice and zest. Set aside.

3   Cut the bananas in half lengthwise and arrange them in a shallow baking dish (an oval gratin dish works well). Pour on the sugar syrup and dot with bits of the margarine. Sprinkle with cashews and coconut and bake for 20 minutes, basting occasionally. Serve garnished with the reserved lime twists.

Blushing Poached Pears

SERVES: 4

INGREDIENTS

- 1½ cups cranberry juice
- 1 cup sugar
- 2 teaspoons pure vanilla extract
- ripe Bosc or D'Anjou pears
- 2 scoops of vegan vanilla ice cream
- Chocolate Sauce, homemade or store-bought
- Mint sprigs, for garnish

INGREDIENTS

1. Lightly grease a 9 x 13-inch baking pan and set it aside. Preheat the oven to 400°F. In a large saucepan, combine the cranberry juice and sugar over medium heat.

2. Cook, stirring, until the sugar dissolves, then bring to a boil over medium-high heat. Continue to boil for 8 minutes, then remove from the heat and stir in the vanilla.

3. Peel the pears and cut them in half lengthwise. Scoop out the cores with a melon baller and arrange them in the prepared pan. Pour the cranberry syrup over the pears, turning to coat. Bake until just tender, but not falling apart, about 30 minutes.

4   Remove from the oven and cool to room temperature, then refrigerate until chilled. When ready to serve, arrange 2 of the pear halves on each of 4 chilled dessert plates, spooning any remaining syrup over the pears. Nestle a scoop of ice cream on each plate. Drizzle each with the chocolate sauce and garnish with a mint sprig.

Grilled Orange And Strawberry Skewers

SERVES: 4

INGREDIENTS

- 2 large navel oranges, peeled and cut into 1-inch chunks
- large ripe strawberries, hulled
- ½ cup Grand Marnier or other orange-flavored liqueur

DIRECTIONS

1   Skewer the orange chunks and strawberries on 8 skewers, placing 2 or 3 orange chunks on each skewer, followed by 1 strawberry, and finishing with 2 or 3 pieces of orange.

2   Place the skewered fruit in a shallow dish and pour the Grand Marnier over the fruit, turning to coat. Set aside for 1 hour. Preheat the grill.

3   Grill the fruit skewers, brushing with the marinade, about 3 minutes per side. Serve the skewers hot, drizzled with the remaining marinade.

Rum-Sautéed Pineapple and Bananas With Toasted Coconut And Pecans

SERVES: 4

INGREDIENTS

- ¼ cup vegan margarine
- ½ cup sugar
- ½ pineapple, peeled, cored, and cut into 1-inch chunks
- ¼ cup dark rum
- 2 tablespoons toasted coconut
- 2 tablespoons unsalted toasted pecans, coarsely chopped

DIRECTIONS

1   In a large skillet, heat the margarine and sugar over medium heat. Cook, stirring, until the sugar dissolves, about 2 minutes.

2   Add the pineapple and bananas and cook for 1 to 2 minutes. Carefully add the rum and simmer until the alcohol cooks off for about 2 minutes.

3   Spoon into 4 dessert dishes and sprinkle with coconut and pecans.

Nellie's Peachy Melba

SERVES: 4

INGREDIENTS

- 2 cups water
- ripe peaches
- 1½ cups sugar
- 2 tablespoons plus 1 teaspoon lemon juice
- 1 cup fresh raspberries
- 2 scoops of vegan vanilla ice cream
- 1 tablespoon sliced toasted almonds

DIRECTIONS

1   In a large saucepan, bring the water to a boil over high heat and add the peaches. After 30 seconds, reduce the heat to medium, scoop out the peaches with a slotted spoon, and place them in a bowl of cold water.

2   To the simmering water, stir in 1 cup of the sugar and 2 tablespoons of the lemon juice, stirring to dissolve the sugar. Reduce the heat to low and keep the water at a simmer while you remove the skins from the peaches.

3   Remove the skins from the cooled peaches and return the peaches to the simmering water for 8 minutes. Drain the peaches, then pit and slice them. Set aside.

4   In a small saucepan, combine the raspberries and the remaining ½ cup of sugar and heat over medium heat.

5   Crush the berries with the back of a spoon to release the liquid, stirring to dissolve the sugar. Press the berries through a fine sieve into a bowl to remove the seeds. Discard the seeds. Add the remaining 1 teaspoon of lemon juice and set aside.

6   Scoop the vegan ice cream into clear dessert bowls and top with the sliced peaches. Drizzle with the raspberry sauce, sprinkle with almonds and serve.

Asian Flavors Fruit Bowl

SERVES: 4

INGREDIENTS

- 1 (8-ounce) can lychees, packed in syrup
- Juice of 1 lime
- 1 teaspoon lime zest
- 2 teaspoons sugar
- ¼ cup water
- 1 ripe mango, peeled, pitted, and cut into ½-inch dice
- 1 Asian pear, cored and cut into ½-inch dice
- 2 bananas, peeled and cut into ¼-inch slices
- 1 kiwifruit, peeled and cut into ¼-inch slices
- 1 tablespoon crushed unsalted roasted peanuts

DIRECTIONS

1 Drain the lychee syrup into a small saucepan and place the lychees in a large bowl and set aside.

2 Add the lime juice and zest to the lychee syrup, along with the sugar and water, and heat over low heat until the sugar dissolves. Bring to a boil and remove from heat. Set aside to cool.

3 To the bowl containing the lychees add the mango, pear, bananas, and kiwifruit. Drizzle with the reserved syrup, sprinkle with peanuts and serve.

Sweet Polenta With Grilled Pineapple And Strawberry Sauce

SERVES: 4

INGREDIENTS

Polenta

- 2 cups water
- ¾ teaspoon salt
- 1 cup medium yellow cornmeal
- ¼ cup sugar
- 2 tablespoons vegan margarine
- 1 tablespoon canola or other neutral oil

Topping

- ¼ cup sugar
- 2 cups hulled strawberries
- 1 teaspoon fresh lemon juice
- 1 pineapple, peeled, cored, and cut into ½-inch slices

DIRECTIONS

1   Make the polenta: Bring the water to a boil in a large saucepan. Reduce the heat to medium, add the salt, and slowly stir in the cornmeal. Reduce the heat to low, stir in the sugar and margarine, and continue to cook, stirring frequently, until thick, about 15 minutes.

2   Spoon the polenta into a greased shallow baking dish and refrigerate until firm, at least 30 minutes. Preheat the oven to 375°F.

3   Cut the polenta into serving-size pieces and arrange them on a greased baking sheet. Brush the tops with the oil and bake until hot and golden brown, about 20 minutes.

4   Make the topping: In a food processor, combine the sugar, 1 cup of the strawberries, and lemon juice, and blend well. Transfer to a small serving bowl and set aside. Preheat the grill. Cut the remaining strawberries into thin slices and set them aside. Grill the pineapple slices on both sides until grill marks appear.

5   Arrange a serving of the polenta on each plate, place the grilled pineapple on top, drizzle with the strawberry sauce, and scatter the strawberry slices overall.

Pineapple Couscous Timbales with Blueberry Sauce

SERVES: 6

INGREDIENTS

- 2 cups pineapple juice
- 1 cup couscous
- ½ cup crushed pineapple, drained
- 1 tablespoon light brown sugar
- ½ teaspoon ground cinnamon
- Blueberry Sauce, homemade or store-bought

DIRECTIONS

1   Lightly oil 6 timbale molds and set aside. In a medium saucepan, bring the pineapple juice to a boil over high heat. Add the couscous, pineapple, sugar, and cinnamon. Reduce the heat to low, cover, and simmer until the juice is absorbed about 5 minutes.

2   Press the couscous mixture into the prepared molds and refrigerate for at least 1 hour.

3   Unmold the timbales and place each on a dessert plate, surround with a pool of the blueberry sauce, and serve.

Lime-Macerated Mangos

SERVES: 6

INGREDIENTS

- ripe mangos
- ⅓ cup sugar
- 2 tablespoons fresh lime juice
- ½ cup dry white wine
- Fresh mint sprigs

DIRECTIONS

1. Peel, pit, and cut the mangos into ½-inch dice. Layer the diced mango in a large bowl, sprinkling each layer with about 1 tablespoon of the sugar. Cover with plastic wrap and refrigerate for 2 hours.

2. Pour in the lime juice and wine, mixing gently to combine with the mango. Cover and refrigerate for 4 hours.

3. About 30 minutes before serving time, bring the fruit to room temperature. To serve, spoon the mango and the liquid into serving glasses and garnish with mint.

MEDITERRANEAN SEAFOOD

Dad's Mussels

SERVES: 4

INGREDIENTS

- o   kg mussels
- 3-4 large onions, cut in rings
- 50 g   butter
- 1 pkg   mussel spice (ready-mix)
- 1 cup   water
- cups white wine
- salt and pepper (to taste)
- bunch of parsley
- lemon slices

DIRECTIONS

1   Water and clean mussels. Take them out of the water.
2   Take a large pot (5 l or about 1 gallon) and melt 50 g butter. Add water, wine, mussel spices, salt, and pepper. Boil shortly and add the drained mussels.
3   Boil about 10-20 minutes. Shake the pot several times during the cooking time. The mussels are ready when all of the mussels have opened. Add parsley when the cooking is finished.
4   Serve with slices of lemon and slices of toasted white bread.

Oysters grilled with roasted garlic butter and romano

SERVES: 4

INGREDIENTS

- 1 cup (2 sticks) unsalted butter, cut into pieces
- cup Grill-Roasted Garlic mashed
- Rubbing
- teaspoons Creole Rub
- dozen large oysters, shucked
- 1 tablespoon fresh lemon juice
- cups grated Romano cheese
- tablespoons chopped fresh
- lemon wedges
- parsley

DIRECTIONS

1. Combine the butter, Creole rub, lemon juice, parsley, and mashed roasted garlic in a small saucepan. Cook over medium heat until the butter is no longer foaming and has started to brown slightly about 5 minutes.

2. Light the grill for direct medium heat, about 375¼F. Brush and oil the grill grate. Place the oysters directly on the grate and top each with about 2 teaspoons of the sauce and 1 tablespoon of the cheese.

3. Grill until the oyster shells char and the cheese melts and browns around the edges, about 8 to 10 minutes.

4. Remove the oysters to a heat-proof platter or tray. Drizzle another teaspoon of the sauce over each oyster and serve hot with the lemon wedges for squeezing.

Baked Oysters with Bleu Cheese

SERVES: 4

INGREDIENTS

- 1/2 pound peeled young potatoes
- tablespoons milk
- tablespoons olive oil
- tablespoons chopped flat–leaf parsley
- dozen plump, fresh oysters
- Salt and pepper, to taste
- egg yolks
- tablespoon dry white wine
- 2/3 cup cream
- ounces crumbled bleu cheese

DIRECTIONS

1. Cook the potatoes in salted, boiling water until tender. Drain well, and mash (using a fork) together with the milk, olive oil, and parsley.
2. Open the oysters, separate the bodies from the shell, keep the juice, and set aside. Throw away the top shell, and wash the bottom shell thoroughly.
3. Beat the egg yolks together with the wine, and put in a double boiler to cook until the mixture doubles in volume, continuing to beat during cooking.

4. In another pan, mix the cream and the Bleu cheese. Bring to a boil for 2 to 3 minutes, then remove from heat. Add the oyster juice, and fold this mixture gently into the egg yolks.

5. To serve, fill the oyster shells with the mashed potatoes. Put the oysters on top, and cover with the sauce. Put them under the grill for 5 minutes so that the mixture becomes golden brown.

6. Serve hot.

Barbecued Oysters

SERVES: 4

INGREDIENTS

- cups oysters
- 3/4 cup flour
- Seasoned salt and pepper, to taste
- 1 1/2 cups barbecue sauce

DIRECTIONS

1 Drain oysters well.

2 Mix flour, salt, and pepper in a brown grocery bag. Shake oysters in fa lour mixture.

3 Sauté oysters in hot oil just enough to form a crust, but not enough to completely cook.

4 Place oysters in an oblong baking dish and cover oysters with barbecue sauce.

5 Bake at 350 degrees F for 20 to 25 minutes.

Fried Oysters

SERVES: 1

INGREDIENTS

- 11-pint oysters, drained
- Salt and cayenne pepper, to taste
- Cup All–purpose flour
- Cup Yellow cornmeal OR Masa Harina (corn flour)

DIRECTIONS

1   Sprinkle the oysters with salt and cayenne pepper.

2   Mix the flour and cornmeal (or cornflour) until combined evenly.

3   Roll the seasoned oysters in the flour and set them aside on waxed paper.

4   Heat oil in a large pot or deep fryer to 375 F.

5   Deep fry oysters in batches until golden, about 2 minutes. Do not overcrowd, Do not overcook. Serve immediately.

Oysters Johnny Reb

SERVES: 10

INGREDIENTS

- 2 quarts oysters, drained
- 1/2 cup finely chopped parsley
- 1/2 cup chopped scallions
- 2 tablespoons lemon juice
- 1/2 cup butter or margarine, melted
- 2 cups fine cracker crumbs
- 1 tablespoon Worcestershire sauce
- Salt and pepper, to taste
- Tabasco® sauce
- Paprika
- 6 tablespoons milk
- 6 tablespoons light cream

DIRECTIONS

1   Place a layer of oysters at the bottom of a greased, shallow, 2–quart baking dish. Sprinkle 1/2 each of the parsley, onions, lemon juice, butter, crumbs, Worcestershire, salt, pepper, and Tabasco over oysters,

2   Make another layer of the same.

3   Sprinkle with paprika.

4   Just before baking, make evenly spaced holes in the oyster mixture.

5   Pour milk mixed with cream into holes, being careful not to moisten crumb topping all over.

6   Bake at 375 degrees F for 30 minutes or until firm.

Oysters Rockefeller

SERVES: 10

INGREDIENTS

- tablespoons butter
- tablespoons raw spinach chopped fine
- tablespoons parsley chopped fine
- tablespoons celery chopped fine
- tablespoons onion, chopped fine
- cups fine dry bread crumbs
- Few drops of Tabasco sauce
- 1/2 teaspoon salt
- 1/2 teaspoon Pernod or anisette
- 36 oysters on the half shell
- Rock salt

DIRECTIONS

Melt butter in a saucepan and stir in all ingredients except oysters and rock salt.
Cook over low heat, stirring constantly, for 15 minutes.

Work through a sieve or food mill and set aside.

Make a layer of rock salt in pie tins and place oysters on top. Put a teaspoonful
of the vegetable mixture on each oyster. Broil under a preheated 400 degrees F
broiler for 3 to 5 minutes or until topping begins to brown. Serve immediately in
the pie tins.

Pan-fried Oysters

SERVES: 4

INGREDIENTS

3 dozen small fresh oysters, shucked

1/3 cup flour, or more

1 cup ground soda crackers (30)

2 eggs

6 tablespoons butter, divided into thirds

3 tablespoons vegetable oil

DIRECTIONS

Drain oysters, then blot oysters to dry on paper toweling. Place flour and cracker crumbs on separate sheets of wax paper.

Beat eggs slightly in a mall bowl. Dredge oysters in flour; dip into egg, then in crumbs, pressing crumbs to adhere. Place on a wax paper—lined baking sheet.

Heat 2 tablespoons butter and 1 tablespoon oil in a large, heavy skillet over medium—high heat just until butter is melted. Add a third of the oysters and sauté for 2 minutes until golden brown. Turn over and sauté for another 2 minutes. Remove to a paper towel—lined tray. Empty skillet and wipe clean. Repeat frying in 2 batches with the remaining oysters.

Scalloped Oysters

SERVES: 4

INGREDIENTS

- 1-pint oysters
- 1/2 cup oyster liquor (the liquid oysters are sold in)
- tbsp. light cream
- 1/2 cup white bread crumbs
- 1 cup cracker crumbs
- 1/2 cup melted butter
- Salt
- Pepper

DIRECTIONS

1   Preheat oven to 400F.
2   Mix bread and cracker crumbs with melted butter. SA spread a thin layer of crumbs on the bottom of a released shallow baking dish.
3   Cover with half of the oysters, sprinkle with salt and pepper and add half of cream and oyster liquor. Repeat layers, and cover top with crumbs. Bake for 30 minutes.
4   If you increase the quantities, use a larger dish and still only two layers.

Corn Bread Fried Oysters

SERVES: 4

INGREDIENTS

- 1 1/2 cups yellow cornmeal
- 1/2 cup all-purpose flour
- eggs, lightly beaten
- cups milk
- 1/4 cup melted bacon fat or butter
- 1 tablespoon baking powder
- 1/2 teaspoon salt
- cups peanut oil, for deep-frying
- 36 freshly shucked oysters
- Lemon wedges, as an accompaniment

DIRECTIONS

1   In a medium bowl, combine the cornmeal, flour, eggs, milk, bacon fat, baking powder,and salt. Stir until the batter is smooth.

2   In a large saucepan or deep-fryer, heat the oil to 375F. Dredge each oyster in the cornmeal batter and fry in batches until golden brown, about 1 minute.

3   Remove the oysters with a slotted spoon and drain on paper towels. Serve with lemon wedges.

Thai-style Mango Salad with Griddled Prawns

SERVES: 4

INGREDIENTS

- 20 large, headless tiger prawns
- 4 skewers
- 1 thumb-sized piece fresh ginger, grated 20g pack fresh coriander, chopped
- 1 red chili, deseeded and chopped
- 4 tablespoons fresh lime juice
- 3 tablespoons olive oil
- 1 tablespoon sesame oil
- 1 tablespoon soy sauce Good pinch of brown sugar
- 1/2 clove garlic, peeled and crushed
- 1 ripe and ready-to-eat mango
- 2 handfuls ready-to-eat bean sprouts
- 3 small cucumbers, chopped
- 1 handful fresh coriander
- 1 red pepper, deseeded and cut into thin strips
- 1 bunch spring onions, chopped
- Sea salt
- A small handful of sesame seeds
- Bianconi extra virgin olive oil, to drizzle

DIRECTIONS

1 Slide 5 peeled prawns onto each skewer.

2 For the marinade, mix the ingredients and drizzle half over the prawns. For the salad, peel the mango and cut the flesh into thin strips.

3 Mix with the other half of the marinade, bean sprouts, cucumber, coriander, pepper, spring onions, and sea salt.

4 Heat a large frying pan and dry-fry the sesame seeds until golden. Remove and set aside. Fry the prawns over high heat for 2 minutes until cooked through.

5 Serve with the salad, sprinkled with sesame seeds, and drizzled with olive oil.

Spicy Thai Curry

SERVES: 4

INGREDIENTS

- ½x 5ml spoon ground cumin or if using a whole seed, then pound or crushed
- 1 heaped 5ml spoon ground coriander or (if using a whole seed then pound or crushed)
- 2-3 fresh whole green chilies to your taste
- 4 large thumb-sized pieces of fresh ginger, peeled and chopped 3 fresh lemongrass stalks, trimmed back, and chopped
- 4 cloves garlic, peeled
- 4 handfuls of fresh coriander with stalk attached
- 6 salad onions, washed and trimmed
- 2 limes, zest of one, and juice of both 30ml spoon olive oil, to loosen 400ml can coconut milk
- 200g fine green beans, tailed
- 200g baby corn
- 2-3 x 15ml spoons light or dark soy sauce or fish sauce if preferred 300g chilled or frozen cooked prawns, tiger prawns, or king prawns

DIRECTIONS

1   Place the first 10 curry paste ingredients into a food processor and whiz up to a fine paste for 1 minute. In a hot wok or casserole-type pan pour in a little oil, add the curry paste, and cook for 30-40 seconds.

71

2   Next, add the coconut milk and simmer for 3 minutes before adding the green beans and baby corn.

3   Simmer for a further 7 minutes then season with soy sauce finally adding the prawns.

4   Remove from the heat and serve immediately with some lightly fluffy fragrant rice.

Pesto-stuffed prawns with guacamole vinaigrette

SERVES: 4

INGREDIENTS

- prawns or colossal (10Ð15 count)
- shrimp
- 1jalapeno chile pepper, seeded
- cup Cilantro Pesto
- tablespoons chopped shallot
- tablespoons olive oil
- 1 small garlic clove, minced
- tablespoons chopped fresh cilantro
- Rubbing
- Guacamole Vinaigrette:
- teaspoon coarse salt
- Hass avocados, pitted and peeled
- Pinch of ground black pepper
- Juice of 1 large lime   cup extra-virgin olive oil
- 1 tomato, seeded and finely chopped

DIRECTIONS

1   Light a grill for direct medium-high heat, about 425¼F.

2   Slit the prawns along their backs to open up the center crevice slightly. Fill the opening in each prawn with about ½ to 1 teaspoon pesto. Coat the stuffed prawns all over with olive oil.

3   For the guacamole vinaigrette: Mash the avocado in a medium bowl with a fork. Stir in the remaining ingredients. Set aside.

4   Brush the grill grate and coat with oil. Grill the prawns directly over the heat until firm and nicely grill-marked, about 4 minutes per side.

5   Remove to plates and drizzle with the guacamole vinaigrette.

Tempura Prawns

SERVES: 4

INGREDIENTS

- 120g Tempura flour
- 200ml Iced water (add ice cubes)
- 500ml sunflower or vegetable oil
- 2 Shiitake mushrooms
- 4 fresh king prawns
- ¼sweet potato
- 1 carrot
- ¼ aubergine
- 2 green beans
- 2 slices pumpkin

DIRECTIONS

1   Wash your vegetables: cut the sweet potato and pumpkin into slices, carrot into batons and aubergine into fans; Leave the prawns, shiitake, and green beans Dry them with a paper towel and place in the fridge to chill

2   Make the batter: mix 120g of tempura flour with 200ml of ice-cold water (use ice cubes)

3   Heat approximately 3 inches of oil in a pan, wok or deep fat fryer to 160-170 degrees

4   Dust each ingredient with flour, dip into the batter and drop into the heated oil
5   Use wooden chopsticks to turn the ingredients so they cook evenly
6   Once lightly golden, remove and drain on kitchen paper
7   Serve tempura dipping sauce and curry powder whilst still hot!

MEDITERRANEAN PASTA

Pasta Sausage Skillet

PREP TIME: 5 Minutes

COOKING TIME: 30 Minutes

SERVES 4

INGREDIENTS

- 1/2 lb.. lean ground beef
- 2 celery ribs, sliced
- 1/4 lb.. bulk Italian sausage
- 4 oz. uncooked spaghetti, broken in half
- 2 (8 oz.) cans of no-salt-added tomato sauce
- 1/4 tsp dried oregano
- 1 (14 1/2 oz.) cans stewed tomatoes
- salt and pepper
- 1 C. water
- 1 (4 oz.) can mushroom stems and pieces,
- drained

DIRECTIONS

1   Place a pan over medium heat. Brown in it the sausage with beef for 8 min. Discard the fat.

2   Stir in the rest of the ingredients. Cook them until they start boiling. Put on the lid and let them cook for 15 to 17 min.

3   Serve your pasta pan warm. Garnish it with some chopped herbs.

4   Enjoy.

NUTRITIONAL VALUES

Calories 400.4, Fat 15.6g, Cholesterol 58.4mg, Sodium 805.7mg, Carbohydrates 42.2g, Protein 22.9g

Gilroy Garlic Spaghetti

PREP TIME: 20 Minutes

COOKING TIME: 40 Minutes

SERVES 2

INGREDIENTS

- 8 oz. spaghetti
- fresh ground black pepper
- 1 raw egg
- red pepper flakes
- 5 -8 cloves garlic, peeled and press
- vegetarian bacon bits
- 4 tbsp butter
- parmesan cheese
- 1/4-1/3 C. grated parmesan cheese
- black pepper
- 1 tsp dried sweet basil leaves
- 1/4 C. chopped parsley

DIRECTIONS

1   Prepare the pasta by following the instructions on the package until it becomes dente.

2   Get a food blender: Combine in it the egg, garlic, butter, grated Parmesan cheese and dried sweet basil. Blend them smooth to make the sauce 3. Get a serving bowl: Toss in it the pasta with the garlic sauce.

3   Adjust the seasoning of the spaghetti sauce. Serve it with some garlic bread.

NUTRITIONAL VALUES

Calories 730.8, Fat 30.8g, Cholesterol 165.0mg, Sodium 441.9mg, Carbohydrates 88.9g, Protein 23.8g

30-Minute Spaghetti Skillet

PREP TIME: 15 Minutes

COOKING TIME: 30 Minutes

SERVES 4

INGREDIENTS

- 1 lb.. ground turkey
- 1/2 tsp red pepper flakes
- 2 garlic cloves, minced
- 8 oz. uncooked spaghetti, broken into thirds
- 1 small green pepper, chopped
- parmesan cheese
- 1 small onion, chopped
- 2 C. water
- 1 (28 oz.) jars traditional style spaghetti
- sauce

DIRECTIONS

1   Place a large saucepan over medium heat. Cook in it the turkey with garlic, onion, and green pepper for 8 min.

2   Add the water with hot pepper flakes, spaghetti sauce, a pinch of salt and pepper.

3 Cook them until they start boiling. Add the spaghetti to the pot.

4 Bring it to a rolling boil for 14 to 16 min or until the pasta is done.

5 Get a mixing bowl:

6 Enjoy.

NUTRITIONAL VALUES

Calories 486.6, Fat 12.5g, Cholesterol 80.4mg, Sodium 515.2mg, Carbohydrates 60.4g, Protein 32.1g

Autumn Vegetable Roast

PREP TIME: 45 Minutes

COOKING TIME: 120 Minutes

SERVES 6

INGREDIENTS

- 1 spaghetti squash
- 1/2 tsp dried oregano
- 1 large carrot, sliced on the diagonal
- 1 pinch ground allspice
- 2 stalks celery, sliced on the diagonal
- 3 garlic cloves, chopped
- 1 large yellow onion, diced
- 3/4 lb.. part-skim mozzarella cheese
- 1 red bell pepper, peeled, seeded and
- 1/2 C. grated parmesan cheese

- diced
- Oil
- 2 tbsp extra virgin olive oil
- 28 oz. tomatoes, diced, peel, and seed)
- red pepper flakes, minced
- 1 tsp dried basil

DIRECTIONS

1   Put a large pot of water over high heat. Add to it the whole squash and let it cook until it starts boiling.

2   Put on the lid and keep it boiling for 55 min.

3   Place a large pan over medium heat. Heat in it a splash oil. Cook in it the onion with a carrot for 6 min.

4   Stir in the rest of the celery with bell pepper, pepper flakes, a pinch of salt and pepper.

5   Cook them for 12 min while stirring them often. Stir in the remaining ingredients.

6   Let the sauce cook for 16 min over low heat. Add the mozzarella with parmesan cheese.

7   Turn off the heat.

8   Drain the squash from the water. Slice it in half and let it cool down completely.

9   Discard the seeds. Use a fork to scrape the squash pulp.

10 Before you do anything, preheat the oven to 350 F. Grease a casserole dish with a cooking spray.

11 Lay half of the spaghetti squash in the greased casserole. Spread over it half of the cheesy 82

12 Autumn Vegetable Roast

13 veggies mixture.

14 Repeat the process with the remaining mixture. Place the casserole in the oven and let it cook for 32 min.

15 Allow the spaghetti casserole to sit for 5 min then serve it warm.

16 Enjoy.

NUTRITIONAL VALUES

Calories 285.7, Fat 16.6g, Cholesterol 43.7mg, Sodium 515.7mg, Carbohydrates 16.2g, Protein 19.3g

Homemade Chinese Hot and Sour Soup

PREP TIME: 5 Minutes

COOKING TIME: 15 Minutes

SERVES 1

INGREDIENTS

- 1 (3 oz.) packages ramen noodles
- 2 C. water
- 1/8 C. mushroom, thinly sliced
- 1 tbsp rice vinegar
- 1/8 tsp chili sauce
- 1 egg, beaten
- 1/8 C. meat, cooked, sliced thinly. (optional) 1 green onion, light and dark green parts,
- sliced thin

DIRECTIONS

1   In a pan, add 2 C. of the warm water, ramen noodles, and mushrooms and bring to a boil.

2   Add the rice vinegar and chili sauce and cook for about 5-7 minutes.

3   Reduce the heat to medium.

4   Add the sliced meat and stir to combine.

5 Very slowly drizzle, add the beaten egg, stirring continuously.

6 Divide the soup into serving bowls and serve hot with a sprinkling of the sliced onion.

NUTRITIONAL VALUES

Calories 466.2, Fat 19.5g, Cholesterol 211.5mg, Sodium 1078.4mg, Carbohydrates 57.6g, Protein 14.7g

Full Indonesian Stir Fry

PREP TIME: 15 Minutes

COOKING TIME: 35 Minutes

SERVES 4

INGREDIENTS

- 2 (3 oz.) packages ramen noodles (any
- 2 tbsp oil
- flavor, discard flavor packet)
- cooking spray
- 2 C. cooked chicken breasts (cut into strips)

FOR SAUCE

- 2 tbsp sambal oelek, or sriracha
- 1 C. carrot, cut into matchstick-sized pieces 2 tbsp rice vinegar 1/4 lb. fresh sugar snap pea, trimmed and
- 2 tbsp sugar
- string removed
- 2 tbsp soy sauce
- 5 scallions, sliced
- 3 tbsp water
- 1 C. peanuts, chopped (divided)
- 1 tsp lime juice
- 1 (14 oz.) cans bean sprouts, rinsed and
- 1 tsp Thai fish sauce
- drained

- 1/4 tsp sesame oil

- 1 tsp minced garlic

- 1 tbsp cornstarch

- 2 eggs

DIRECTIONS

1 Break each ramen noodle square into 4 portions.

2 In a pan of salted boiling water, cook the noodles for about 2-3 minutes.

3 Drain the noodles and rinse under cold water. Again, drain well.

4 In a bowl, add all the sauce ingredients and mix till well combined.

5 Heat a large greased skillet on medium-high heat.

6 Break the eggs and cook till just cooked, stirring continuously.

7 Transfer the scrambled eggs to a plate and keep them aside.

8 With the paper towels, wipe out the skillet.

9 In the same skillet, heat the cooking oil and stir fry the carrots and sugar snap peas for about 2-3 minutes.

10 Add the scallions and 2/3 of the peanuts and stir fry for about 1 minute.

11 Add bean sprouts and garlic and stir fry for about 1 minute.

12 Full Indonesian Stir Fry

13 With a spoon, push all ingredients to the outside edges of the skillet.

14 Add the ramen noodles and Stir fry for about 1 minute.

15 Add the chicken and sauce mixture and cook till heated through.

16 Stir in the scrambled eggs and cook till heated through.

17 Serve with a topping of the remaining peanuts.

NUTRITIONAL VALUES

Calories 733.1, Fat 40.6g, Cholesterol 164.5mg, Sodium 1231.8mg, Carbohydrates 55.1g, Protein 42.6g

VEGAN MAIN DISHES

Almost One-Dish Thanksgiving Dinner

SERVES: 6

INGREDIENTS

- 2 tablespoons olive oil
- 1 cup finely chopped onion
- 2 celery ribs, finely chopped
- 2 cups sliced white mushrooms
- $\frac{1}{2}$ teaspoon dried thyme
- $\frac{1}{2}$ teaspoon dried savory
- $\frac{1}{2}$ teaspoon ground sage
- Pinch ground nutmeg
- Salt and freshly ground black pepper
- 2 cups fresh bread cubes
- $2\frac{1}{2}$ cups vegetable broth, homemade (see Light Vegetable Broth) or store-bought
- $\frac{1}{3}$ cup sweetened dried cranberries
- 8 ounces extra-firm tofu, drained and cut into $\frac{1}{4}$-inch slices
- 8 ounces seitan, homemade or store-bought, very thinly sliced
- $2\frac{1}{2}$ cups Basic Mashed Potatoes
- 1 sheet frozen puff pastry, thawed

DIRECTIONS

1   Preheat the oven to 400°F. Lightly oil a 10-inch square baking dish. In a large skillet, heat the oil over medium heat.

2   Add the onion and celery. Cover and cook until softened, about 5 minutes. Stir in the mushrooms, thyme, savory, sage, nutmeg, and salt and pepper to taste. Cook, uncovered, until the mushrooms are tender, about 3 minutes longer. Set aside.

3   In a large bowl, combine the bread cubes with as much of the broth as needed to moisten (about

4   1½ cups). Add the cooked vegetable mixture, walnuts, and cranberries. Stir to mix well and set aside.

5   In the same skillet, bring the remaining 1 cup broth to a boil, reduce heat to medium, add the tofu, and simmer, uncovered, until the broth is absorbed about 10 minutes. Set aside.

6   Spread half of the prepared stuffing in the bottom of the prepared baking dish, followed by half of the seitan, half of the tofu, and half of the brown sauce. Repeat layering with the remaining stuffing, seitan, tofu, and sauce.

Seitan Milanese with Panko And Lemon

SERVES: 4

INGREDIENTS

- 2 cups panko
- ¼ cup minced fresh parsley
- ½ teaspoon salt
- ¼ teaspoon freshly ground black pepper
- 1 pound seitan, homemade or store-bought, cut ¼-inch slices
- 2 tablespoons olive oil
- 1 lemon, cut into wedges

DIRECTIONS

1   Preheat the oven to 250°F. In a large bowl, combine the panko, parsley, salt, and pepper. Moisten the seitan with a little water and dredge it in the panko mixture.

2   In a large skillet, heat the oil over medium-high heat. Add the seitan and cook, turning once, until golden brown, working in batches, if necessary.

3   Transfer the cooked seitan to a baking sheet and keep warm in the oven while you cook the rest. Serve immediately, with lemon wedges.

Sesame-Crusted Seitan

SERVES: 4

INGREDIENTS

- ⅓ cup sesame seeds
- ⅓ cup all-purpose flour
- ½ teaspoon salt
- ¼ teaspoon freshly ground black pepper
- ½ cup plain unsweetened soy milk
- 1 pound seitan, homemade or store-bought seitan, cut into ¼-inch slices
- 2 tablespoons olive oil

DIRECTIONS

1   Place the sesame seeds in a dry skillet over medium heat and toast until lightly golden, stirring constantly, 3 to 4 minutes. Set aside to cool, then grind them in a food processor or spice grinder.

2   Place the ground sesame seeds in a shallow bowl and add the flour, salt, and pepper, and mix well.

3   Place the soy milk in a shallow bowl. Dip the seitan in the soy milk, then dredge it in the sesame mixture.

4   In a large skillet, heat the oil over medium heat. Add the seitan, in batches if necessary, and cook until crisp and golden brown on both sides, about 10 minutes. Serve immediately.

Pan-Seared Seitan With Artichokes And Olives

SERVES: 4

INGREDIENTS

- 2 tablespoons olive oil
- 1 pound seitan, homemade or store-bought, cut into ¼-inch slices
- 2 garlic cloves, minced
- 1 (14.5-ounce) can diced tomatoes, drained
- 1½ cups canned or frozen (cooked) artichoke hearts, cut into ¼-inch slices
- 1 tablespoon capers
- 2 tablespoons chopped fresh parsley
- Salt and freshly ground black pepper
- 1 cup Tofu Feta (optional)

DIRECTIONS

1   Preheat oven to 250°F. In a large skillet, heat 1 tablespoon of the oil over medium-high heat. Add the seitan and brown on both sides, about 5 minutes.

2   Transfer the seitan to a heatproof platter and keep warm in the oven.

3   In the same skillet, heat the remaining 1 tablespoon oil over medium heat. Add the garlic and cook until fragrant, about 30 seconds.

4   Add the tomatoes, artichoke hearts, olives, capers, and parsley. Season with salt and pepper to taste and cook until hot, about 5 minutes. Set aside.

5   Place the seitan on a serving platter, top with the vegetable mixture, and sprinkle with tofu feta, if using. Serve immediately.

Seitan With Ancho-Chipotle Sauce

SERVES: 4

INGREDIENTS

- 2 tablespoons olive oil
- 1 medium onion, chopped
- 2 medium carrots, chopped
- 2 garlic cloves, minced
- 1 (28-ounce) can crush fire-roasted tomatoes
- ½ cup vegetable broth, homemade (see Light Vegetable Broth) or store-bought
- 2 dried ancho chiles
- 1 dried chipotle chile
- ½ cup yellow cornmeal
- ½ teaspoon salt
- ¼ teaspoon freshly ground black pepper
- 1 pound seitan, homemade or store-bought, cut into ¼-inch slices

DIRECTIONS

In a large saucepan, heat 1 tablespoon of the oil over medium heat. Add the onion and carrots, cover, and cook for 7 minutes.

Add the garlic and cook 1 minute. Stir in the tomatoes, broth, and the ancho and chipotle chiles. Simmer, uncovered, for 45 minutes, then pour the sauce into a blender and blend until smooth. Return to the saucepan and keep warm over very low heat.

In a shallow bowl, combine the cornmeal with salt and pepper. Dredge the seitan in the cornmeal mixture, coating evenly.

In a large skillet, heat the 2 remaining tablespoons of oil over medium heat. Add the seitan and cook until browned on both sides, about 8 minutes total. Serve immediately with the chile sauce.

Seitan Piccata

SERVES: 4

INGREDIENTS

- 1 pound seitan, homemade or store-bought, cut into ¼-inch slices
  Salt and freshly ground black pepper
- ½ cup all-purpose flour
- 2 tablespoons olive oil
- 1 medium shallot, minced
- 2 garlic cloves, minced
- 2 tablespoons capers
- ⅓ cup white wine
- ⅓ cup vegetable broth, homemade (see Light Vegetable Broth) or store-bought
- 2 tablespoons fresh lemon juice
- 2 tablespoons vegan margarine

- 2 tablespoons minced fresh parsley

DIRECTIONS

1   Preheat the oven to 275°F. Season the seitan with salt and pepper to taste and dredge in the flour.

2   In a large skillet, heat 2 tablespoons of the oil over medium heat.

3   Add the dredged seitan and cook until lightly browned on both sides, about 10 minutes. Transfer the seitan to a heatproof platter and keep warm in the oven.

4   In the same skillet, heat the remaining 1 tablespoon oil over medium heat. Add the shallot and garlic, cook for 2 minutes, then stir in the capers, wine, and broth.

5   Simmer for a minute or two to reduce slightly, then add the lemon juice, margarine, and parsley, stirring until the margarine is blended into the sauce. Pour the sauce over the browned seitan and serve immediately.

672 - Three-Seed Seitan

SERVES: 4

INGREDIENTS

- ¼ cup unsalted shelled sunflower seeds
- ¼ cup unsalted shelled pumpkin seeds (pepitas)
- ¼ cup sesame seeds
- ¾ cup all-purpose flour
- 1 teaspoon ground coriander
- 1 teaspoon smoked paprika
- ½ teaspoon salt
- ¼ teaspoon freshly ground black pepper
- 1 pound seitan, homemade or store-bought, cut into bite-size pieces
- 2 tablespoons olive oil

DIRECTIONS

1   In a food processor, combine the sunflower seeds, pumpkin seeds, and sesame seeds and grind to a powder.

2   Transfer to a shallow bowl, add the flour, coriander, paprika, salt, and pepper, and stir to combine.

3   Moisten the seitan pieces with water, then dredge in the seed mixture to coat completely.

4   In a large skillet, heat the oil over medium heat. Add the seitan and cook until lightly browned and crispy on both sides. Serve immediately.

Fajitas without Borders

SERVES: 4

INGREDIENTS

- 1 tablespoon olive oil
- 1 small red onion, chopped
- 10 ounces seitan, homemade or store-bought, cut into ½-inch strips
- ¼ cup canned hot or mild minced green chiles
- Salt and freshly ground black pepper
- (10-inch) soft flour tortillas
- 2 cups tomato salsa, homemade (see Fresh Tomato Salsa) or store-bought

DIRECTIONS

1   In a large skillet, heat the oil over medium heat.

2   Add the onion, cover, and cook until softened, about 7 minutes. Add the seitan and cook, uncovered, for 5 minutes.

3   Add the sweet potatoes, chiles, oregano, and salt and pepper to taste, stirring to mix well. Continue to cook until the mixture is hot and the flavors are well combined, stirring occasionally for about 7 minutes.

4   Warm the tortillas in a dry skillet. Place each tortilla in a shallow bowl.

5   Spoon the seitan and sweet potato mixture into the tortillas, then top each with about ⅓ cup of the salsa. Sprinkle each bowl with 1 tablespoon of the olives, if using. Serve immediately, with any remaining salsa served on the side.

Seitan with Green Apple Relish

SERVES: 4

INGREDIENTS

- 2 Granny Smith apples, coarsely chopped
- ½ cup finely chopped red onion
- ½ jalapeño chile, seeded and minced
- 1½ teaspoons grated fresh ginger
- 2 tablespoons fresh lime juice
- 2 teaspoons agave nectar
- Salt and freshly ground black pepper
- 2 tablespoons olive oil
- 1 pound seitan, homemade or store-bought, cut into ½-inch slices

DIRECTIONS

1   In a medium bowl, combine the apples, onion, chile, ginger, lime juice, agave nectar, and salt and pepper to taste. Set aside.

2   Heat the oil in a skillet over medium heat.

3   Add the seitan and cook until browned on both sides, turning once, about 4 minutes per side.

4   Season with salt and pepper to taste.

5   Add the apple juice and cook for a minute until it reduces. Serve immediately with the apple relish.

COOKING CONVERSION CHART

TEMPERATURE		WEIGHT	
FAHRENHEIT	**CELSIUS**	**IMPERIAL**	**METRIC**
100 °F	37 °C	1/2 oz	15 g
150 °F	65 °C	1 oz	29 g
200 °F	93 °C	2 oz	57 g
250 °F	121 °C	3 oz	85 g
300 °F	150 °C	4 oz	113 g
325 °F	160 °C	5 oz	141 g
350 °F	180 °C	6 oz	170 g
375 °F	190 °C	8 oz	227 g
400 °F	200 °C	10 oz	283 g
425 °F	220 °C	12 oz	340 g
450 °F	230 °C	13 oz	369 g
500 °F	260 °C	14 oz	397 g
525 °F	270 °C	15 oz	425 g
550 °F	288 °C	1 lb	453 g

MEASUREMENT			
CUP	ONCES	MILLILITERS	TABLESPOON
1/16 cup	1/2 oz	15 ml	1
1/8 cup	1 oz	30 ml	3
1/4 cup	2 oz	59 ml	4
1/3 cup	2.5 oz	79 ml	5.5
3/8 cup	3 oz	90 ml	6
1/2 cup	4 oz	118 ml	8
2/3 cup	5 oz	158 ml	11
3/4 cup	6 oz	177 ml	12
1 cup	8 oz	240 ml	16
2 cup	16 oz	480 ml	32
4 cup	32 oz	960 ml	64
5 cup	40 oz	1180 ml	80
6 cup	48 oz	1420 ml	96
8 cup	64 oz	1895 ml	128